SELFIES FROM THE BACKSEAT

DURRA

Made with ♥ on the Notion Press Platform
www.notionpress.com

To You.

Contents

Contents

Acknowledgements

Directly and indirectly this book is a result of a lot of people, efforts and experiences. No regrets; all gratitude.

First and foremost, everlasting thanks to Shrutika Nagpal, for believing, supporting and being an all-out spirited person. You have been a supremely supportive, true force of monumental relentlessness. I hope you realise I am forever going to be indebted to you, financially, mentally and emotionally.

My mumma, Dr. Roshvi Shinde, to whom no number of acknowledgements would do justice. You gave me life. Simply by that extension of gratitude, my words are as much as my efforts as they are hers. Thank you, Mom, for your never-ending confidence in me. I hope I made you proud. I forever love you.

Mr. Vishwashyam Khamamkar, my best mate, my Mount Vesuvius or as I call him, Vishuvious, a brother from another mother. Thank you for your perspectives, conversations and inside jokes in the darkest times. You have no right to be such a blatant realist while being a devil's advocate but you do a brilliant job of it; never change.

Janhavi K. for your inputs and brainstorms, along with proofreading and looking after the hygiene of my first baby, this piece of work.

I know I have still skipped important names, but if you know me like you do, you know who you are; precious.

Lastly, you, the reader, for investing your time and money to keep a part of me with you in the form of this book, thank you.

Preface

For a long time, writing has been my ability and my disability because of the way it was used with insincere and thoughtless conviction based on what I wanted to express.

The alter ego, Durra (pronounced du-*ra*), found his voice in making love and the longing to make love.

Spanning over half a decade, this journey of its main characters You and I, who are stuck in a twisted knot of fate, where neither breaking away nor holding on makes any logical or practical sense, starts in the evening before either knew of the other's existence, until they meet at eventide, flowing and ebbing into each other soon after midnight, as finally, twilight dawns on them, You, the girl, and I, the boy, and these are their Selfies from the Backseat, which capture a series of those mental snapshots that expose You & I at their most vulnerable, naïve and naked best, along with Fate, Destiny and Love sometimes making guest appearances, in the pictures, peeking their heads through the door of their lives, only to shut it behind them before You & I could make it to the same room to hold each other, before You & I could touch the creases and lines of each other's bodies, before You & I could accumulate enough memories to internalise each other for a lifetime, although, the jury of the Gods is still out on whether You & I will be successful or not but their love, lovemaking and the longing to make love is an outright success, as at its worst, it is melancholic and at its best, it's exuberant, living on in multitudinous proportions as you will soon understand, as you read between the lines and then reread, attempting to make sense of their ordeal, of their entanglement, of them trying to find a sliver of relief and a glimmer of hope, just as you did, do or will do, before submitting against Fate and Destiny, living to fight another battle, another day, but today, when you turn a new leaf, remember to wish yourself a happy new day, today and every day, because you not only made it this far but also because you made it here, to have me in your hands and in your mind, agreeing to be a spectator to my exhibition with private pictures of You & I being intimate, provocative and sensuous; smile wide for me now, all teeth.

Evening

The sunset; dusk.

1. I, The Wristbreaker

In the company of a dusty, dingy old
ceiling fan with a small red bulb
in a dimly lit room,
sitting with a bottle of rum,
some music and a brooding view.
I try to make sense of life,
sense of the sound of rain,
sense of the grey in the concrete,
sense of the silence in my soul.
I write about
all that I have seen
and met
and known.
"You are a writer of chaos,
a connoisseur of pain
who uses his words to cut and slash.
Making up stories that strain
the boundaries of truth and
limits of art".
I have seen it all, in the dark by-lanes,
the seedy bars,
the broken dreams, and
the mental scars
of a city that never sleeps, and
of the people that it never forgives.

And I write of it all,
with a scorching burning passion
that lives,
for writing is my escape,
a way to make sense
of this world
that's falling apart and breaking.
In the emptiness of my dimly lit room,
I find silence in the words I write,
spinning the stories I chase;
be warned and wary
of such a writer of the dark
who turns pain into art
in a city that never sleeps,
writing of the darkness and the
dreams, so that you may sleep.

2. You, an Art

In the company of a fragrant, crisp cornucopia
of pungent and woody perfumes,
she sits with a pashmina scarf,
a missing smile and wild dreams envisioned.
She loves black but paints in colour
with brushes bold and strokes that cover
the fabric as if a thin tight rubber.
She loves her art and in turn,
it loves her.
Her muse is not only a ray of light,
it's the textures that evoke feelings
you did not know
you could feel anymore.
She loves the haunting time of night
when she is the glitter
that is difficult to get off
once it touches you.
She draws from pain and squeezes the tube
to find freedom again
in the shape of truth and
all its hues.
She wears her black as if a cloak that
shields her from fate and
its silly cruel joke.

A blank canvas is a temple
made of her deepest parts,
untouched and divine.
A blank canvas is a battleground
where she lets her soul run wild.
A blank canvas is where the demons
come out in colourful harmony,
like Beethoven playing Für Elise
for the the first time in its original key.
Though the world may attempt to dim
her flames from burning bright,
she is a fierce undying reminder
in the darkness,
that her energy can make us
whole again, in no time.

3. Explore

Before you become someone
who completely
surrenders or submits
to dissolve
into the society
of misplaced dreams
and mourned ambitions
on your way
sleepwalking
to work every day,
getting
domesticated
for debt,
for junk food and
for the compromise
of eating a chicken bucket
while emailing your boss
on the weekend
instead of
getting nostalgically
drunk at a pub
where you aren't
allowed to smoke
and be painfully hungover
the next morning as you woke,

playing back last night's conversation
on how about this
and what if that -
your life would've been
totally different.
If only you explored
to become someone
that somewhat resembled
at least half of the
end product
that you intended
to be.
Is it not worth exploring?

4. Amor Fati

How many people do not get
the one they want
but end up with the one
they are destined to be with?
Fate doesn't change
even if together we are
milk and honey,
my hand on your hip
is not enough to rewrite it.
Fate is not meant to be fair,
it is supposed to be like
being caught in a current
much stronger than we are;
struggle against it and
risk drowning not just yourself
but also, those you are
trying to save.
Destiny, on the other hand,
pushes you to swim,
to survive like dead bodies afloat
going with the flow.
"The universe is supposed to conspire
to make happen every decision
of yours happen.
Ultimately, giving us the power

to change our destiny
but only if we are brave enough
to fight against fate
for what we crave.
Now, this tempter, Destiny,
will definitely make its way around
to sucker punch us
right across the face.
We need to get back up each time
to learn to love Destiny and
fuck Fate in the face again".

5. Fighter, Loser

In my last dream,
I was swimming towards
the sunset.
Every stroke made
was an attempt to blend
into the blue sky,
into the blue ocean,
with a blue me.
And then in a wink,
washing out colours,
the sun set on me,
leaving behind
a sore,
black and blue
defeated me.

6. Coil

This is so much more
than I could ever handle or give:
A life free of lies and
a meaningful relationship.
With hands pinned down at the sides waiting for
the end of the aching in the guts,
the end of this high fever and
the feverish dream
which keeps a heightened focus
on bodies that painted
a portrait of adultery.
The ticklish taste of
the reason I breathed,
her tongue, our fate
is now building a vice-like
grip to choke me.

7. Conversation with Dark

Into the dark of the night,
I whisper, "Who owns this love which lives in me?"
"I do, but together with you", you replied.
"So, is this you shattering those mirrors?"
"Merely a reflection, like
how the indigenous inhabitants of a
cosmopolitan once resembled each other".
Adamant, "But there is someone else here too.
Who is it?"
"A prisoner, our wounded soul"
"A love this dangerous
won't let it off easy", winking,
holding on to the thread
but not breaking it,
sharing it like how
the lips and the tongue play
with the words we speak
that are housed within,
not imprisoned like the soul,
in this sanctuary of our simple and
dangerous love.
Pulling the thread for everything other than keeping you away
in the darkness,
when I rub my eyes,
and look again,

"With love, my Love",
the evening whispers
back to me in the darkness.

8. Hi? Hi.

"Have we loved someone?"
"You have said I love you,
and I love you
has often been the reply back".
"Is it the attraction to my appearance this time?
or
do you pick on my brain too?"
With time, the conversation
goes on for months,
decades even,
and there really is
no real end.
Referencing back
and forth
and fifth
and sixth
to seventy
inside, sort of,
trivia, jokes and limericks
that thrived
as consequence of
the relationship.
The 'I love you'
becoming a deletable affectation.

The length of the conversations,
a lifeline.
"What is your number
of disconnected hotlines?"
"Seventh, eighth, ninth, tens",
tensed,
"How do we choose to hang on?
How do we choose to cordially end?"

9. Rough Metaphors

"Since You and I met, we are
no longer two".
Like the unrelenting glaze
in the eyes of a doe
trapped under the claws of a lion.
Like what happens to the sun
when its rays break through
the window onto bodies.
No. Longer. Two.
The ocean waves are our closest likeness,
the wind currents closest to our unity,
the sandstorms closest to our intricacies.
This combination of You & I
is a oneness
like the apparent separation
of rays.
In reality, we are so overcome,
so dissolved into each other,
all qualities of lonesomeness disappear.
We have nothing to do with existence
or doubling down on our investments,
we fly without any wings,
talk without any words,
with the world on our shoulders
when we jump up on the scale

opposite eternity,
claiming to balance it;
till a sigh of relief,
one that's too deep,
trips the triple beam balance.

10. Knot Noted

Knots are probably the most mastered human skill.
From macrame baskets to modern surgery,
hafted on stones with sinew and bones
to being adorned on ankles and
sashayed across torsos and toes,
knots are the ubiquitous
musical notes of labour, life and love.
Would we then prefer
our strings breaking, withering
or
should we be tying them back up
with better mastery at work
since before recorded history?
Clothing, cordages for home,
fishnets and funerals, knots fit all.
Do you then not know
to not unknot a knot?
Do note that we cannot knot
a donut, because everything knots,
a circle does not
unless you really know to knot
the sound of a butterfly effect
early in its infancy to
cause a twist of fate.

Eventide

The light between dusk and night

11. Chances

When I came back to this life,
asking strangers for directions,
petrified, with a map
inscribed on my palm,
you said your heart had healed
and that left a tiny crack in mine
along an ancient fault line.
What kind of four-leaf clover am I?
A lucky charm for everyone but myself.
You probably knew this already
because my eyelashes
told you everything I couldn't say,
with all their insistent fluttering.
"Loving a soul that is taken
leaves room for an imagination
that wants to kiss
your singing mouth on a street,
show you off to everyone I meet,
paint you in my sleep,
make your body moan,
turn up the heat",
whispered the Moon to the tides,
"Come a little closer tonight
fill me up with an
intricate spiderweb of lullabies

laced through your mouth,
flood me,
when I sleep next to you
and wake up on a riverbed
loveless and dry"
Growing up in a disintegrating home,
they try to build theirs intact
with her first moves
and his love spells
which keeps reacquainting them with
homesickness.

12. Battle Ready

On a diet of smoke and solvents,
when I watch these wheels spinning
sometimes I wonder how am I still alive?
Then I look at her and I get my answer
to the most beautiful question in my mind,
that I still frame, like a still frame
nailed and hanging on a wall
by a thread,
our reins holding our tongue,
eyes, ears, skin and nose,
as this chariot of our bodies
is set ablaze.
She is a drug
that takes you in and away
before that last fix to show you
addiction is a monster
that never sleeps
even if, you,
the driver of this chariot,
is mindful of its passengers' spirit,
the longing,
the exhaustion and
the explosion
from her eyes is enough to
perish it.

13. Suicide Spectacle

She has the capacity
to be the diary that
I confide to
recite my life in.
This precious,
special one
even replies to me
through her own
precious,
special
eyes courting death
causing
an optical tsunami.
This precious,
special one
I'm going to kamikaze in.

14. Parched And Quenched

In the kitchen
sitting on the platform
with her legs crossed,
with her eyes shooting daggers
for the uninformed.
Thirsty
throat
wants
water.
Hungry
desires
want
thunder.
No wants,
just
that
one want.
You could hear it,
their sexual tension loud and clear,
as if they are already fucking
while he was just still
trying to find the nerve
to simply touch her once
like the right swipe scroll
he did to her picture

on his phone.
Tapping barefoot rhythmically,
she is home,
now as the exciting music,
playing as the background score;
the sound of the ground
is tap dancing around the
conversations slicing
through their minds.
"What if she never left?
What if the thirst never quenched?",
a question forever left
unanswered.

15. The Beauty In

"My state of mind is You".
She is the centre of attention,
the sound that starts from the teeth and lip,
and travels lip to lip,
back to the teeth and lip,
in a linear symmetry,
a pretty face-fuck.
The rule is do not try.
If you do try, go all the way.
Gorging in the nightmarish
insides of a cafe,
the queasy uneasy messy meal
was sweat and dirt.
Without being in the same room as her
unlocking imaginations
and a lifetime together
running wild like beasts
simplified for reality,
exploding with beauty;
fingers photorealistic.
Expectations set in stone,
multidimensional snapshots
captured onto one.
Hung high, walking tall;
Portrait of my Feisty Girl.

16. Clock Vice

Once I had to be somewhere
but I was late.
It's been so long
but I'm still running late.
Always
screaming and
screaming
for time but never
for punctuality,
I lie,
waiting
like an animal
that deserves to be put down.
Finally,
it is
about
time.

17. Theatrics

The many moods that you can make me feel;
The many moods that you can make me express.
Despite animosity between us,
I see the joy in your eyes,
still, through the screen
looking back at me every time
as if an incredible audience
wants me centre stage,
and here I am
under your brow,
facing your sight
under the spotlight
of your eyes.
You.
Lost in you, blended, burning out,
I want to keep you
while soaking
deeper within you
like cloth in Molotov burning out
the cocktail before being flicked off
to a spot where I will continue to exist,
sinking deeper within the skin
like a birthmark,
like a burn mark.

Seeing you fully bloom
in pictures,
whereas in reality slipping
through the fingers
like the floral dress
around your waist,
intoxicating and drug laced.
The one with a pseudonym,
the one with a
flickering untamed flame.
Everything's about You.
Memories of eventide whisper,
"Darling, I should never let you go".

18. Looking Back

The strangest
most hateful nights
come while
sitting alone
and looking back
at the bastard
I was younger and
more open to dreaming
carefree.
Looking back,
it all couldn't have
been much better.
What a lovely
fucking time
it was.

19. The Sky Above

Should we ever feel
lonely or alone,
let's never mistake
the attention we get
for love and care;
attention doesn't appease
to our will of longing and
belonging, and to the
design of that darling
dopamine
called Love.
Resorting to being
someone's moonlight
at noon,
without affecting the
existing cover of
the sky above
and between
the horizon and the serene view,
this silent, expansive gesture
is worth its weight
in celestial space.

20. Sowing Time

The shadows cast are
a proof that the
sun still shines,
but even the sun
needs a place to hide.
I want mine in my own clouds.
I want control of my own sky
because everything is dark
even when
the stars twinkle,
the moon's bright
and it is midnight.

Midnight

The beginning and end

21. Inauguration

Everything has a start and an end.
A grand miraculous life.
A small powerful sentence.
Collectively, paragraphs become
too intense,
too thick to memorize,
too meticulous to rote,
too mindful to recall
like those people we forget.
A memorable sentence dissolves like water and salt.
In a world full of paragraphs
I was looking for my life sentence,
my better half
who completes me
each day with a lifetime
of sentences, one for
each day.
No-one knows the beauty
of a beginning and an end
more than
the artists, writers and the poets
consumed in a sentence;
with awareness of the tensions
between lineation and syntaxes
of all beginnings and ends.

22. Happy New Day

It happens every day, every time,
the moment the eyes open
and I wake up.
Moments later,
after inveigling myself into believing
what's the point in reminiscing
when I am trying to forget it all?
Although unsuccessfully
since it's the rap
that I took
that is the most painful;
not all its accompanying memories.
"So, rejoice and reminisce,
but do not be stuck in the
consequence".
I tell myself,
"it's one day at a time".
Yesterday ended at midnight,
today is always right now
and just like that
tomorrow never comes.
It's one day at a time.
"Happy new day, my Milky Way",
the midnight whispers back to me.

23. Bleed

People have come and gone,
they are still coming and going.
Women have come and gone,
they are still coming and going.
I remember
the silver linings
stemming like arteries
flowing with heartbreaks and romances
with those one-off chances,
the hits and misses
all of whom eventually blending into
one sort of an organ
for that eventual fateful one,
made of all these
wants and nots and
do's and don'ts
miraculously cancelled out by
trial and error,
and an "oh yes",
as fate would have said,
this organ is now beating in my hand
with a thorn in its side
which when I pull,
everything collapses and dies.

24. Shooting Stars

I request my asteroid
to dent me a
crater as a home
when the menace of the Universe
enters Mother Earth
on a suicide mission
disregarding its inner light
for mutual redamancy
of two nyctophiles.

25. Circling Inferno

We don't need relationships,
we have inner heretic gods
to feed the devotion
of the love behind the hell doors.
Like you are Cerberus and
I'm the bones he crushed.
Like you are Persephone and
I'm Hades clovening through
our kingdom underground
that we rule,
rarely exiting;
together in this bottomless perdition
engulfed in fiery sweetness.
Paradise found in you.

26. Chasing Heights

Everything is half done,
like the delirium of a drunk,
hiding behind the bottle,
fighting troubles,
I fought mine covered in a white
blanket,
chasing the colourless dragons
trying to complete a mystical trip,
fix after fix,
trigger before the treat,
cramming the puzzle pieces
to make it fit,
as a whole I was scared,
as if someone someday
would see me from afar
and say,
"Wow, what a beautiful painting,
it's incomplete, what a shame".

27. Snapshot of an Unlocked Cage

Something has changed you completely.
You look exactly the same wonderful
person, day after day,
who used to come down to my house,
down to fuck
while standing, laying down and bent over.
You were hungry, sophisticated, affectionate
even then,
You were the most
unspoiled soul in the whole world.
Now, I don't know what has become of you.
You talk with
a newfound fire,
a glint of it in your eye.
"It is all that darned hound from hell,
Love's influence", I see that.
It is a thrilling and thriving
tale of romance and survival
in a fascinating blend
of love, life and lore,
which makes art insanity,
which makes love, a malady and
which makes nirvana
the greatest orgasm of your life.

Pushing faith and fact to the limit,
like hounds that are controlled
by canes and whips,
thinking of you,
thinking like you,
wherever you are right now
reading this,
and threads snap;
and you lose your way in the labyrinth.
How bad of fall will it be?
How deep of a rock bottom this time?
Have you simply made it a habit
of the cold loneliness at the bottom?
"A tiny cut can be explained,
not a potential lifelong scar
but with such a nice frame
it would be a shame not to hang it".
Odd that you want to get nailed
but nails are off the table,
railed but trained to hide
track marks from your arms.
No number of slaps and pinches
will wake you from this dream now,
these are absolutely necessary
for her art and his mastery.

28. Offing

I will always be
all yours,
you will never be
all mine.
Two heartbeats beating.
Two souls existing
but not combined.
On that thin ice,
doing the dance of death,
pressed pause when
felt her breath
leaving me breathless
now I'm not going anywhere
except suicidal
giving back my life to its rightful.
The horseman in his stride,
Death's spokesperson,
won't see me crying in the rain
but instead dying in the deep ocean
this time around
I won't swim,
I will float,
going with the flow
unburdened from the tiredness
of a lifetime

falling, falling, falling
eternally in the abyss,
black as the night.
Death outliving life.

29. Congregation

Falling raindrops like tears of love,
they were both,
the one that adored and
the one that adores
the divided hearts
roaring with love
through space and time
discounting fate and its dealing hand
Is this love or a memory that has last?
Is this their heart beating or failing fast?
Is this love or a spell that's cast?
Even in the parting, their love never dies.
Even in the goodbyes, their love is alive
their bond carries on
in their longing across walls
flying, giving wings to their love,
but fate that day had other plans
and decided to blow their wicked disguise,
when they gazed from the stars and
the sky above,
these falling raindrops
their moment had come and
passed them by
onward to an unknown destination
it flowed,

leaving them behind
as memories in
the rivers of their life.

30. Sleep

I cannot sleep.
Soon morning will come,
people will rise again
after all the darkness
to walk their way to work.
I'll be at my window
touching my clouds
passing by my day
under a grey, melancholic sky
when I will be writing
chapters of bad novel on
a bad day with sunrays
slapping across my face
like a smile
at twilight.

Twilight

The illumination before sun rises

31. Indestructible

Their passionate affair
is only 2 inches away:
secret, private
and always within reach
but she has promises
to keep
before she can lie in bed
cajoling her ducts to not weep.
Rising from her
bitter end,
clandestine and condemned,
are thoughts of sadness
converging from his to
her head.
With days as hard
as the ceiling,
with no shards sharp enough
to rip them apart,
she idolises
being dead.

32. Passion in a Cage

He might not see anything in her
but she notices everything in him,
a new manner, new patterns,
certain new lines
in shades of loneliness
and subtleties,
in shapes of daydreams and nightmares,
whose mere memories
adds colour to her cheeks,
rouge, red, crimson
like the path in forest
in the middle of autumn
at around midnight, laden with blood
dripping from a sharp canine,
the animal within will have never felt
more alive.

33. Chivalrous Adultery

They both love the same album
but separately and strongly,
she enjoys different songs off it.
Yet she plays it like he wants,
when in the morning,
the man teases the woman in bed.
"Please stop, not in front of the kid.",
filled with unpleasant anger, she says.
They share a smoke.
They share a smile.
She questions what's killing her more,
before getting up and out,
shaking her behind,
she walks to the kitchen
and sings a popular song,
of which she has forgotten the lines
meaningless lyrics combined
with an affectionate tone
in a calm, soothing voice,
she starts cooking for the man's
post lunch belches.
In the afternoon, the man goes out.
The woman rushes back to him,
the one lingering
in her mind

with their legs and arms
entwined.
It's the same hum
this time
now dressed in its Sunday best,
like two children left
playing in the park
with candies to last the day
before their weekend's spent.

34. Seeking Life

Well now,
If little by little
you stopped loving me
I shall have never stopped loving you.
Little by little,
if suddenly you forget me
and then looked for me, at me,
I shall never have forgotten you.
If we think long and hard
and decide to discard
everything in the winds that pass through life,
that love, it will never fade.
It will never go away,
as long as one of us hangs on to it,
that love makes the both of us immortal.
If little by little,
getting demoted from a priority
to an option,
left at the shore
where the heart has taken roots,
remember
that on any day, at any hour,
in a hot minute,
I shall beat again
and my roots will seek you.

It is fragile for sure
maybe that's why
hearts are meant to be
broken too.

35. Gaslit

I want a
part of you,
you never could
part with.
Outside, inside,
under my nails,
in my gut churning,
burning whatever
I am, that remains incomplete.
Insomniac
of the year,
the fire within me could never
let me
sleep in bed
with everything
I don't have,
not knowing
what
to do
to save myself.
Doused and smeared
in forgotten love,
I light myself up
to put on a show
for two familiar strangers

in a madhouse of
pain,
as for being
with you
is as simple
as it is
complicated.

36. Live, Love, Die

Life isn't scary;
it's its persistent movement
when the ultimate aim is nothing.
Love isn't scary;
it's its many meanings
or lack thereof.
Death isn't scary;
it's where you end up
before it happens.

37. Over the Horizon

Two lovers, fire in a bottle,
endless romance of licks and roars
doing a tempestuous dance of a
wildfire when their hands explore
like the water between land and shore,
as lines get ignored
in the distance, a shimmering mirage
of the border between light and dark,
a horizon of hope
when the sun rises,
it is a magic trick,
a price paid by darkness to elope
unlike their fiery love in a bottle
with a lid on top,
veiled and maintained;
their burning passion
sealed and contained.

38. With You

Twisting and turning
with you,
while sleeping next to you,
dreaming about
the aromas
from the field of flowers
that fill my holes and pores
like it is you
back home
when I am not looking for you
anymore
but instead
looking at you
back in bed
when you don't leave
anymore
but instead
pull me back in
with you
pushing me back on my back
to ride me to glory,
to kingdom come,
with legs clearly
pointing to different
parts of hell.

What an orgasmic dream it was,
you should've seen us.

39. Journeying

I wish we could always remain,
text messages in a chat window,
but instead
we remained
a tank full of gas,
an empty road,
and nowhere to go.

40. Royalties of the End

Sometimes I wonder
if things would always
remain so uncertain,
so unclear,
so wide open
like the hole
where my home used to be,
where you used to be;
now the hole is what I fall in
to end up living my days and
nights and in my loneliest times,
when I watch the world fall apart
staring back blank
at me,
at my failure
that seeks freedom
from a monster named Fate
bedding insanity,
questioning, whether one person
can be two things at once?
oil and water,
the one you love and
the one who loves you
on an arduous journey
from being

indispensable to expendable
pulling you deeper than deep
back in time
like a time machine
convincing you that
maybe the Gods got it right,
we reincarnate each time.
I know this for a fact because
on one of those days
when I wake up alone
with worlds apart,
with no one next to me to
call a home
and emptiness sunk deep
in my bones,
that otherwise blinds my reality,
switches off my brain to
mentally not be present anywhere
by tiring out my muscles
when I would turn my fear
into a fake laugh
that now,
suddenly seems sincere
and then, now when I ask,
"where are you?"
"Washing your scents",
you reply in unison
with the twilight.
What an end to have. Bye.

Epilogue

I have forgotten how to write as myself. It doesn't instinctively kick in like it used to, when I was in front of a blank page with a pen in hand. Even as I am writing this, writing is purposeful. The voice, the tone, the punctuation, are expressions. Under a pseudonym, it isn't entirely me - the one who wrote diaries that spoke to him, and were for his eyes only. Now, none of my words are exclusively mine. They are for the world to interpret, pick apart and react to. It's sticky territory. And then there is You, in front of whom I'm at my most naked; mentally stripped down from all the fancy bells and whistles, and the accessories to the crime of being tactfully honest that I commit otherwise. I'm not guilty about my words with you or for you. I am me, as I am with myself with You in my head. That is my love for You and my way of showing it.

This is not a love note about that though. Because I can't be writing a convincing love note without being brutally honest with You about what I feel about myself, You and then, us. I don't want us to get to that today, right now, in this moment, while I also don't want to paint You a paragraph that is simply seen with rose-tinted glasses. I know we love each other. I know we love making love to each other. And I also know we long to make love to each other. That is what I think about us, in a capsule. But alas, we don't exist in isolation. We are a part in a growing and maturing world, with which we too grow and mature.

Everything I have ever written to You is without a filter between the mind and the mouth. But I do have to go through the filters each time before I tell You something that I really want to tell You, instead of saying something that would distract or appease You, 'cuz that's what those filters do: tell people what they want to hear, instead of what I want to say. That is also why I hold on to You, being this shamelessly vehement. As cliched as it may sound, I like myself when I am with You. That's why you have my permission to live in my head, not tentatively as a tenant, but as a house spouse (coining it) in my mind's home.

Unfortunately, I only ask for something from You that You can't give me in a satisfying bulk, but instead, only in doses small enough for me to continue being hooked on to You, as if love is the dealer and dopamine, is the drug. You, a high. Hi? Hi. I wish we could be together too. Yet somehow, we still are and aren't. We are Schrodinger's love. That's the clutch I walk with, I'm getting rosy again, jeez. I'm going to pluck this right here. I miss you, always. Thanks for making time for me.

Kisses.

Printed by Libri Plureos GmbH in Hamburg,
Germany